JUNE 2011

Death Investigation: A Guide for the Scene Investigator

Technical Update

Original Guide Developed and Approved by the
National Medicolegal Review Panel

Executive Director
Steven C. Clark, Ph.D.
Occupational Research and Assessment, Inc.
Big Rapids, Michigan
Associate Professor
Ferris State University
November 1999

Technical Update Developed and Approved by the
Technical Update Review Committee
March 2010
U.S. Department of Justice
Office of Justice Programs

The original project was supported under grant number 96–MU–CS–0005 by
the National Institute of Justice, Office of Justice Programs, U.S. Department
of Justice, and by the Bureau of Justice Assistance and the Centers for
Disease Control and Prevention.

The technical update was supported under grant number 2007–MU–BX–
K008 by the National Institute of Justice, Office of Justice Programs, U.S.
Department of Justice.

NCJ 234457

Original Guide: National Medicolegal Review Panel

The National Medicolegal Review Panel (NMRP) represents a multidisciplinary group of content area experts, each representing members of his or her respective organization. Each organization has a role—be it active involvement or oversight—in conducting death investigations and in implementing these guidelines.

United States Conference of Mayors
The Honorable Scott L. King (Chairman, NMRP)
Mayor
Gary, Indiana

American Academy of Forensic Sciences
Joseph H. Davis, M.D.
Retired Director, Dade County Medical Examiner Department
Miami, Florida

American Bar Association
Bruce H. Hanley, Esq.
Partner, Hanley & Dejoras, P.A.
Minneapolis, Minnesota

American Medical Association
Mary E.S. Case, M.D.
Chief Medical Examiner
St. Louis, St. Charles, Jefferson, and Franklin Counties, Missouri

St. Louis University School of Medicine, College of American Pathologists
Jeffrey M. Jentzen, M.D.
Medical Examiner
Milwaukee, Wisconsin

International Association of Chiefs of Police
Chief Thomas J. O'Loughlin
Wellesley, Massachusetts

International Association of Coroners and Medical Examiners
Halbert E. Fillinger, Jr., M.D.
Coroner
Montgomery County, Pennsylvania

National Association of Counties
Douglas A. Mack, M.D., M.P.H.
Chief Medical Examiner and Public Health Director
Kent County, Michigan

**National Association of
Medical Examiners**
*Richard C. Harruff, M.D.,
Ph.D.*
Associate Medical Examiner
Seattle/King County Depart-
ment of Public Health
Seattle, Washington

**National Conference of
State Legislatures**
*Representative Jeanne
M. Adkins*
Colorado State Legislature
House Judiciary Committee
Denver, Colorado

**National Governors'
Association**
*Richard T. Callery, M.D.,
F.C.A.P.*
Chief Medical Examiner
Wilmington, Delaware

**National Sheriffs'
Association**
Donald L. Mauro
Commanding Officer,
Homicide Bureau
Los Angeles County Sheriff's
Department
Los Angeles, California

**Colorado Coroners'
Association**
Elaine R. Meisner
Logan County Coroner
Sterling, Colorado

**South Dakota Funeral
Directors' Association**
George H. Kuhler
Elected Coroner
Beadle County, South Dakota

Technical Update:
Review Committee

American Academy of Forensic Sciences
Julie A. Howe, M.B.A.
Medicolegal Death Investigator
St. Louis University, Division
of Forensic Pathology
St. Louis, Missouri

American Board of Medico-legal Death Investigators
Roberta Geiselhart, R.N.
Supervisor of Investigations
Hennepin County Medical
Examiner's Office
Minneapolis, Minnesota

International Association of Chiefs of Police
Major Rustin Price
Commander, Criminal
Investigation Division
Baltimore County Police
Department
Towson, Maryland

International Association of Coroners and Medical Examiners
O'dell Owens, M.D., M.P.H.
President
Cincinnati State Technical
and Community College
Cincinnati, Ohio

National Association of Medical Examiners
Jeff Jentzen, M.D.
Director of Autopsy and
Forensic Services
University of Michigan
Ann Arbor, Michigan

National Sheriffs' Association
Sergeant Michael Price
DuPage County Sheriff's
Office
Wheaton, Illinois

Acknowledgments

NIJ wishes to thank the original Technical Working Group for Death Investigation (TWGDI). This 144-member reviewer network gave of their time to review guideline content, providing the researcher feedback from a national perspective. Additional thanks to the TWGDI executive board: Mr. Paul Davison, Kent County M.E. Office, Grand Rapids, Michigan; Mr. Bill Donovan, Jefferson Parish Coroner's Office, Harvey, Louisiana; Mr. Cullen Ellingburgh, Forensic Science Center, Orange County, California; Ms. Roberta Geiselhart, R.N., Hennepin County M.E. Office, Minneapolis, Minnesota; Dr. Elizabeth Kinnison, Office of the Chief M.E., Norfolk, Virginia; Mr. Vernon McCarty, Washoe County Coroner, Reno, Nevada; Mr. Joseph Morgan, Fulton County M.E. Office, Atlanta, Georgia; Mr. Randy Moshos, M.E. Office, New York, New York; Mr. Steve Nunez, Office of the Medical Investigator, Albuquerque, New Mexico; Ms. Rose Marie Psara, R.N., St. Louis County M.E. Office, St. Louis, Missouri; and Mr. Michael Stewart, Denver City and County Coroner's Office, Denver, Colorado, whose combined commitment to the field of death investigation is a tribute to the quality of this document. In addition, the offices that employ each member of the group share in this endeavor. Through their support, each member was given the flexibility they needed to support the project.

NIJ also wishes to thank its technical advisors: John E. Smialek, M.D., Chief Medical Examiner, State of Maryland; Randy L. Hanzlick, M.D., Centers for Disease Control and Prevention (CDC) and Emory University School of Medicine; Ms. Mary Fran Ernst, Director of Medicolegal Education, St. Louis University Medical School; and Ms. Mary Lou Kearns, Coroner, Kane County, Illinois. Each made significant contributions to the project's inception, eventual funding, and timely completion. Their dedication to the science of death investigation and to the members of the investigative community is apparent throughout this document.

The former Director of NIJ, the Honorable Jeremy Travis; the Director of NIJ's Office of Science and Technology, Mr. David G. Boyd; and NIJ's Forensic Science Program Manager, Richard M. Rau, Ph.D., each share responsibility for the success of this project. Credit also goes to R. Gib Parrish, M.D., of CDC, for his support of and commitment to the research.

In addition, the true strength of these guidelines is derived from the stamina of the National Medicolegal Review Panel (NMRP), whose members represented 12 national organizations intimately involved in the investigation of death and its outcomes. The panel also included two representatives of elected coroners. NMRP's contribution was invaluable. And finally, thanks go to the leadership of Joseph H. Davis, M.D., Medical Examiner Emeritus, Dade County, Florida, and Mr. Donald Murray, National Association of Counties, for their unrelenting efforts to get this job done and improve their profession, every scene, every time.

In 2010, NIJ convened a committee to perform a technical update to the guidelines. NIJ extends its thanks to the members of the Technical Update Review Committee for their work. NIJ also thanks Ms. Carolyn Allen, Consultant, National Forensic Science Technology Center; Brigid O'Brien, Ph.D., Program Manager, NIJ; and Ms. Robin Jones, Forensic Science Policy and Strategy Consultant, Bureau of Alcohol, Tobacco, Firearms and Explosives, for their assistance in the technical update.

John H. Laub, Ph.D.

Director, National Institute of Justice

Contents

Introduction to Technical Update

Death investigation has evolved greatly in the years since the 1999 release of *Death Investigation: A Guide for the Scene Investigator.* This revised and updated edition is the result of a collaborative effort to present the most up-to-date information about the issues confronting death investigators today. The death investigator is the eyes and ears of the forensic pathologist at the scene. It is hoped that these guidelines, reflecting the best practices of the forensic community, will serve as a national standard.

The following introduction describes the original study that focused on the establishment of guidelines for conducting death investigations.

Introduction to the Original Guide

Purpose and Scope of the Study

The principal purpose of the study, initiated in June 1996, was to identify, delineate, and assemble a set of investigative tasks that should and could be performed at every death scene. These tasks would serve as the foundation of the guide for death scene investigators. The Director of the National Institute of Justice (NIJ) selected an independent review panel whose members represented international and national organizations whose constituents are responsible for the investigation of death and its outcomes. The researcher organized two multidisciplinary technical working groups (TWGs). The first consisted of members representing the investigative community at large, and the second consisted of an executive board representing the investigative community at large.

The study involved the use of two standardized consensus-seeking research techniques: (a) the Developing A Curriculum (DACUM)[1] process and (b) a Delphi[2] survey. In this report, the author does not attempt to assign responsibility for task (guideline) performance to any one occupational job title (e.g., Guideline D4 is performed by law enforcement personnel). Research design and selected methodology focused on the establishment of performance guidelines for death-scene investigations. The research design did not allow TWGs to assume investigative outcomes during the development phase of the project; therefore, no attempt was made to assign a "manner" of death to individual guidelines (e.g., Guideline C2 applies to homicide scenes), to maintain objectivity and national practicality. The author does not claim to be an expert in the science and/or methodology of medicolegal death investigation. This research was based on the collective knowledge of three multidisciplinary content area expert groups. The focus was on the death scene, the body, and the interactive skills and knowledge that must be applied to ensure a successful case outcome. The balance of this introduction outlines the study design and provides basic background information on the selection of the National Medicolegal Review Panel (NMRP) and TWG memberships and the research methodology, its selection, and application.

The study findings (investigative guidelines) follow this introduction.

Study Design

The methodology selected for this occupational research required collection of data from a sample of current subject matter experts, practitioners from the field who perform daily within the occupation being investigated. This "criterion" was used to identify members of the various multidisciplinary groups that provided the data for this research.

The following groups were formed for the purpose of developing national guidelines for conducting death investigations.

National Medicolegal Review Panel

NMRP members represent an independent multidisciplinary group of both international and national organizations whose constituents are responsible for investigating death and its outcomes. Each member of NMRP was selected by the Director based on nominations made by the various associations. The rationale for their involvement was twofold: (a) they represent the diversity of the profession nationally and (b) their members are the key stakeholders in the outcomes of this research. Each organization has a role in conducting death investigations and in implementing these guidelines.

Technical Working Group for Death Investigation

1. National Reviewer Network

Technical Working Group for Death Investigation (TWGDI) members represent a sample of death investigators from across the country. They are the content area experts who perform within the occupation daily. The following criteria were used to select the members of the TWGDI reviewer network:

- Each member was nominated/selected for the position by a person whose name appeared on the most recent (1995) Centers for Disease Control and Prevention (CDC) national database of death investigation.[3]

- Each member had specific knowledge regarding the investigation of death.

- Each member had specific experience with the process of death investigation and the outcomes of positive and negative scene investigations.

- Each member could commit to four rounds of national surveying over a 6-month period.

A 50-percent random sample (1,512) of death investigators was drawn from the CDC database.[4] A letter was sent to each member of the sample, inviting him or her to participate in the national research to develop death investigative guidelines or to nominate a person who participates in death investigations. Two hundred and sixty-three individuals were nominated (17 percent). Nominees were contacted by mail and asked to provide personal demographic data, including job title, years of experience, and educational background, in addition to general information (name, address, etc.) necessary for participation in the research.

The TWGDI national reviewer network consisted of 263 members from 46 states and representing 5 regions, as seen in table 1.

3

The educational backgrounds of the national reviewer network members are presented in table 2.

The types of investigative systems represented in the reviewer network are shown in table 3.

The average age of TWGDI members was 47.6 years. They had an average of 10.5 years of experience. There were 80.6 percent (212) males and 19.4 percent (51) females in the group.

2. Executive Board

Representatives from each region were selected to maintain consistency within regions across the United States. These representatives made up the TWGDI executive board. Criteria for selection to the TWGDI

Table 1. Membership of the Technical Working Group on Death Investigation National Reviewer Network

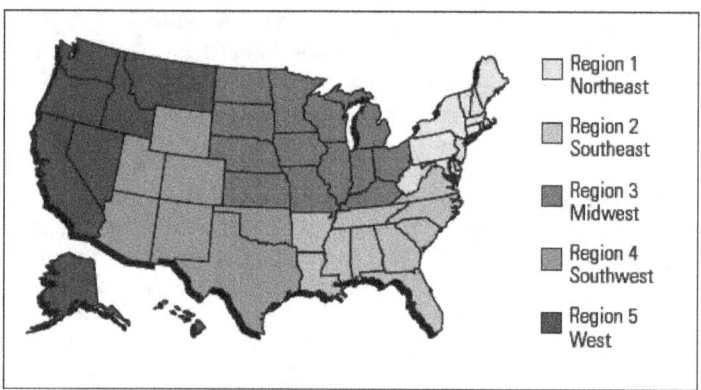

Region	Location	Number of Participants	Percentage
1	Northeast	32	12%
2	Southeast	56	21%
3	Midwest	94	36%
4	Southwest	47	18%
5	West	34	13%

Table 2. Educational Background of the National Reviewer Network

Education	Number	Percent
Law Enforcement	82	31%
Medical	157	60%
Unknown	24	9%

Table 3. Systems Represented by the National Reviewer Network

System	Number	Percent
Medical Examiner	44	17%
Coroner	161	61%
Mixed ME/Coroner	58	22%

executive board were as follows:

- Each member had specific knowledge regarding the investigation of death.

- Each member had specific experience with the process of death investigation and the outcomes of positive and negative scene investigations.

- Each member could commit to attend four workshops held within the grant period.

TWGDI Executive Board DACUM Workshop. In November 1996, the TWGDI executive board met in St. Louis to begin developing the national Delphi survey. The survey content was to reflect "best practice" for death-scene investigation. DACUM is a process for analyzing an occupation systematically. The 2-day workshop used the investigative experts on the executive board to analyze job tasks while employing modified brainstorming techniques. The board's efforts resulted in a DACUM chart that describes the investigative occupation in terms of specific tasks that competent investigators must be able to perform "every scene, every time."[5] A task was defined as a unit of observable work with a specific beginning and ending point that leads to an investigative product, service, or decision. The DACUM chart served as the outline for the Delphi survey.

This initial process resulted in six major areas of work. In attempts to simplify the survey for the members of the national reviewer network, the areas of work were placed into a logical sequence of events (as they might be performed while investigating a case). Within the five major areas of work (Investigative Tools and Equipment was excluded at this point because tools and equipment are "things," not procedural steps), 29 tasks were identified. Within the 29 identified investigative tasks were 149 discrete steps and/or elements. Theoretically, each step and/or element must be performed for the task to be completed "successfully." The results were placed in survey format for NMRP review and pilot testing.

National Medicolegal Review Panel Meeting. In December 1996, NMRP met in Washington, D.C., to review the DACUM chart and comment on the research methodology proposed by the researcher. The members of the panel recommended modifications to the survey design and approved response selections. Respondents would attempt to rate, by perceived importance, each of the investigative tasks/steps and/or elements on a five-point scale.

The Delphi Survey. The Delphi technique, although it employs questionnaires, is much different from the typical questionnaire survey. Developed by the RAND Corporation as a method of predicting future defense needs, the technique is used whenever a consensus is needed from persons who are knowledgeable about a particular subject.[6] The goal of a Delphi survey is to engage the respondents in an anonymous debate in order to arrive at consensus on particular issues or on predictions of future events.

The Delphi survey requires at least four rounds in an effort to obtain a well-thought-out consensus. After the first-round results were received, coded, and recorded, a revised questionnaire was developed for round two. The second-round survey provided each member of TWGDI with the national median and mean scores for each of the task statements presented, as well as their first-round responses. Respondents were asked to compare their original ratings with the median and mean scores and to revise their original evaluations as they saw fit. This procedure was repeated for each of the four rounds of the survey.

The Delphi survey was conducted during the first 6 months of 1997. Table 4 provides general TWGDI response data.

As shown in table 4, final membership in the TWGDI national reviewer network was 146. This number represents approximately 56 percent of the originally nominated members.

Guideline Development. During the 6 months of the Delphi process, both the

TWGDI executive board and NMRP met to review survey data (to date) and to begin the process of moving task-based data into guideline format.

In May 1997, the executive board met for a 2½-day working session in New Orleans to begin the guideline development process. The consensus of the board was to establish 29 guidelines based on the national reviewer network data and present them to NMRP for review. Each guideline would have the following content:

■ A statement of principle, citing the rationale for performing the guideline.

■ A statement of authorization, citing specific policy empowering the investigator.

Table 4. Response Rates to the Delphi Survey

Round	Surveys Sent	Surveys Received	Cumulative Respondent Loss (%)
1	263	199	24%
2	199	163	14%
3	163	149	5%
4	149	146	1%

- A statement of policy to the investigator regarding guideline performance.

- The procedure for performing the guideline.

- A statement of summary, citing justification for performing the procedures.

In June and July 1997, NMRP met for two 1½-day working sessions in St. Louis and Chicago to review the draft guidelines developed by the executive board and offer recommendations and changes based on jurisdictional variances and organizational responsibilities. Those sessions resulted in the final draft of the 29 guidelines for conducting death investigations. The 29 guidelines are presented in the next sections.

Notes

1. The Ohio State University, Center on Education and Training for Employment, DACUM, 1996.

2. Borg, W.R., and M.D. Gall, *Educational Research: An Introduction,* New York: Longman Inc., 1983:413–415.

3. Combs, D., R.G. Parrish, and R.T. Ing, *Death Investigation in the United States and Canada,* Atlanta: U.S. Department of Health and Human Services, Public Health Service, Centers for Disease Control and Prevention, 1995.

4. Ibid.

5. Clark, S.C., Occupational Research and Assessment, Inc., Big Rapids, Michigan, 1996.

6. Borg and Gall, 413–415.

Investigative Tools and Equipment

1. Alternate light source.

2. Barrier sheeting or tent (to shield body/area from public view).

3. Biohazard plastic trash bags.

4. Blood collection tubes.

5. Body bags with locks.

6. Body identification tags.

7. Business cards with fax and e-mail address.

8. Camera equipment.

9. Clean body cover (sheet/drape).

10. Communication equipment.

11. Crime scene tape.

12. Departmental scene forms.

13. Disposable protective suit.

14. Evidence identification markers.

15. Evidence seal/tape.

16. Face and eye protection.

17. First aid kit.

18. Flashlight.

19. Hair cover.

20. Hand tools (e.g., bolt cutter, hammer, metal detector, paint brushes, pocketknife, rope, shovel, etc.).

21. Investigative notebooks.

22 Latent print kit.

23. Latex gloves.

24. Maps, compass and/or GPS.

25. Masks.

26. Measurement instruments.

27. Official identification.

28. Packaging material (e.g., clean unused paper bags, envelopes, metal cans, tape, rubber bands, etc.).

29. Personal supplies (e.g., insect spray, sunscreen, hat, raincoat, umbrella,

boots for wet conditions and construction sites, etc.).

30. Photo identifier (e.g., header frame, placards).

31. Phone lists and contact information.

32. Portable lighting.

33. Recording device.

34. Reenactment doll(s).

35. Resource material (e.g., death scene cleanup, grief support, organ procurement, etc.)

36. Scene safety equipment (e.g., biological/chemical/ industrial/disaster/fire, hardhat, reflective vest, steel bottom boots, etc.).

37. Sharps container.

38. Shoe/boot covers.

39. Specimen containers.

40. Thermometer (ambient and body temperature).

41. Trace evidence recovery equipment (e.g., blades, cotton-tipped swabs, disposable syringe, forceps, gunshot residue and hand lens (magnifying glass), large gauge needles, presumptive blood test kit, scalpel handle, tweezers, etc.).

42. Watch.

43. Waterless hand wash/ disinfectant.

44. Writing instruments.

Arriving at the Scene

1. Introduce and Identify Self and Role

Principle: Introductions at the scene allow the investi-gator to establish formal contact with other official agency representatives. The inves-tigator must identify the first responder to ascertain if any artifacts or contamination may have been introduced to the death scene. The investigator must work with all key people to ensure command protocol and scene safety prior to his/her entrance into the scene.

Authorization: Medical Examiner/Coroner Official Office Policy Manual; State or Federal Statutory Authority.

Policy: The investigator shall take the initiative to introduce himself or herself, identify essential personnel, establish rapport and determine scene safety and security.

Procedure: Upon arrival at the scene, and prior to enter-ing the scene, the investigator should:

A. Identify the lead investigator at the scene and present identification.

B. Identify other essential officials at the scene (e.g., law enforcement, fire, EMS, social/child protective services) and explain the investigator's role in the investigation.

C. Identify and document the identity of the first essential official(s) to the scene (first "professional" arrival at the scene for investigative follow-up) to ascertain if any artifacts or contamination may have been introduced to the death scene.

D. Determine the scene safety and security (prior to entry).

Summary: Introductions at the scene help to establish a collaborative investigative effort. It is necessary to carry identification in the event of questioned authority. It is essential to establish scene safety and security prior to entry.

2. Exercise Scene Safety and Security

Principle: Determining scene safety and security for all investigative personnel is essential to the investigative process. The risk of environmental and physical injury must be removed prior to initiating a scene investigation. Risks can include hostile crowds; collapsing structures; traffic; and environmental, chemical, biological, radiological, nuclear and explosive (CBRNE) threats.

Authorization: Medical Examiner/Coroner Official Office Policy Manual; State or Federal Statutory Authority.

Policy: The investigator shall attempt to establish scene safety and security prior to entering the scene to prevent injury or loss of life, including contacting appropriate agencies for assistance with other scene safety and security issues.

Procedure: Upon arrival at the scene, the investigator should:

A. Assess and/or establish physical boundaries.

B. Identify incident command.

C. Secure vehicle and park as safely as possible.

D. Use personal protective safety devices (physical, biohazard safety).

E. Arrange for removal of animals or secure (if present and possible).

F. Obtain clearance/authorization to enter scene from the individual responsible for scene safety and security (e.g., fire marshal, disaster coordinator).

G. While exercising scene safety and security, protect the integrity of the scene and evidence to the extent possible from contamination or loss by people, animals and elements.

Note: Due to potential scene hazards (e.g., crowd control, collapsing structures, poisonous gases, traffic), the body may have to be removed before scene investigation can be continued.

Summary: Environmental and physical threats to the investigator must be removed in order to conduct a scene investigation safely. Protective devices/equipment must be used by investigative staff to prevent injury. The investigator must endeavor to protect the evidence against contamination or loss.

3. Confirm or Pronounce Death

Principle: Appropriate personnel must make a determination of death prior to the initiation of the death investigation. The confirmation or pronouncement of death determines jurisdictional responsibilities.

Authorization: Medical Examiner/Coroner Official Office Policy Manual; State or Federal Statutory Authority.

Policy: The investigator shall ensure that appropriate personnel have viewed the body and that death has been confirmed.

13

Procedure: Upon arrival at the scene, the investigator should:

A. Locate and view the body.

B. Check for pulse, respiration and reflexes, as appropriate.

C. Identify and document the individual who made the official determination of death, including the date, time and location of determination.

D. Ensure death is pronounced, as required.

Summary: Once death has been determined, rescue/resuscitative efforts cease and medicolegal jurisdiction can be established. It is vital that this occur prior to the medical examiner/coroner's assuming any responsibilities.

4. Participate in Scene Briefing (With Attending Agency Representatives)

Principle: Scene investigators must recognize the varying jurisdictional and statutory responsibilities that apply to individual agency representatives (e.g., law enforcement, fire, EMT, judicial/legal). Determining each agency's investigative responsibility at the scene is essential in planning the scope and depth of each scene investigation and official release of information to the public.

Authorization: Medical Examiner/Coroner Official Office Policy Manual; State or Federal Statutory Authority.

Policy: The investigator shall identify specific responsibilities, share appropriate preliminary information and establish investigative goals of each agency present at the scene.

Procedure: When participating in scene briefing, the investigator should:

A. Locate the staging area (entry point to scene, command post, etc.).

B. Document the scene location (address, mile marker, building name, latitude and longitude coordinates) consistent with other agencies.

C. Determine nature and scope of investigation by obtaining preliminary investigative details (e.g., suspicious versus nonsuspicious death, multiple scenes).

D. Confirm that initial accounts of incident are obtained from the first witness(es).

Summary: Scene briefing allows for initial and factual information exchange. This includes scene location, time factors, initial witness information, agency responsibilities and investigative strategy. **Note:** Since current global positioning system (GPS) devices may have error, it is important to establish the location using other reference points (permanent landmarks) and distance/bearing from landmarks whenever GPS is used.

5. Conduct Scene "Walk Through"

Principle: Conducting a scene "walk through" provides the investigator with an overview of the entire scene. The "walk through" provides the investigator with the first opportunity to locate and view the body, identify valuable and fragile evidence, and determine initial investigative procedures providing for a systematic examination and documentation of the scene and body.

Authorization: Medical Examiner/Coroner Official Office Policy Manual; State or Federal Statutory Authority.

Policy: The investigator shall conduct a scene "walk through" to establish pertinent scene parameters.

Procedure: Upon arrival at the scene, the investigator should:

A. Reassess scene boundaries and adjust as appropriate.

B. Establish a path of entry and exit to include scene log.

C. Identify visible physical and fragile evidence.

D. Document and photograph fragile evidence immediately and collect if appropriate.

E. Locate and view the decedent.

Summary: The initial scene "walk through" is essential to minimize scene disturbance and to prevent the loss and contamination of physical and fragile evidence.

6. Establish Chain of Custody

Principle: Ensuring the integrity of the evidence by establishing and maintaining a chain of custody is vital to an investigation. This will safeguard against subsequent allegations of tampering, theft, planting and contamination of evidence.

Authorization: Medical Examiner/Coroner Official Office Policy Manual; State or Federal Statutory Authority.

Policy: Prior to the removal of any evidence, the custodian(s) of evidence shall be designated and shall generate and maintain a chain of custody for all evidence collected.

Procedure: Throughout the investigation, those responsible for preserving the chain of custody should:

A. Document location of the scene and time of arrival of the death investigator at the scene.

B. Determine custodian(s) of evidence, determine which agency(ies) is/are responsible for collection of specific types of evidence, and determine evidence collection priority for fragile/fleeting evidence.

C. Identify, document, secure and preserve evidence with proper containers, labels and preservatives.

D. Document the collection of evidence by recording its location at the scene, time of collection, and time and location of disposition, and by whom.

E. Develop personnel lists, witness lists, and documentation of times of arrival and departure of personnel.

Summary: It is essential to maintain a proper chain of custody for evidence. Through proper documentation, collection and preservation, the integrity of the evidence can be assured. A properly maintained chain of custody and prompt transfer will reduce the likelihood of a challenge to the integrity of the evidence.

7. Follow Laws (Related to the Collection of Evidence)

Principle: The investigator must follow local, state and federal laws for the collection of evidence to ensure its admissibility. The investigator must work with law enforcement and the legal authorities to determine laws regarding collection of evidence.

Authorization: Medical Examiner/Coroner Official Office Policy Manual; State or Federal Statutory Authority.

Policy: The investigator working with other agencies must identify and work under appropriate legal authority. Modification of informal procedures may be necessary but laws must always be followed.

Procedure: The investigator, prior to or upon arrival at the death scene, should work with other agencies to:

A. Determine the need for a search warrant (discuss with appropriate agencies).

B. Identify local, state, federal and international laws (discuss with appropriate agencies).

C. Identify medical examiner/coroner statutes and office standard operating procedures (discuss with appropriate agencies).

Summary: Following laws related to the collection of evidence will ensure a complete and proper investigation in compliance with state and local laws, admissibility in court, and adherence to office policies and protocols.

Documenting and Evaluating the Scene

1. Photograph Scene

Principle: The photographic documentation of the scene creates a permanent historical record of the scene. Photographs provide detailed corroborating evidence that constructs a system of redundancy should questions arise concerning the report, witness statements or position of evidence at the scene.

Authorization: Medical Examiner/Coroner Official Office Policy Manual; State or Federal Statutory Authority.

Policy: The investigator shall obtain detailed photographic documentation of the scene that provides both instant and permanent high-quality images. It is important to document in writing a description of each photo so that it can be used for future reference.

Procedure: Upon arrival at the scene, and prior to moving the body or evidence, the investigator should:

A. Remove all nonessential personnel from the scene.

B. Obtain an overall orientation photograph of the scene to spatially locate the specific scene to the surrounding area.

C. Photograph specific areas of the scene to provide more detailed views of specific areas within the larger scene.

D. Photograph the scene from different angles to provide various perspectives that may uncover additional evidence.

E. Obtain photographs with scales to document specific evidence.

F. Obtain photographs even if the body or other evidence has been moved.

Note: If evidence has been moved prior to photography, it should be noted in the report, but the body or other evidence should not be reintroduced into the scene in order to take photographs.

Summary: Photography allows for the best permanent documentation of the death scene. It is essential that accurate scene photographs are available for other investigators, agencies and authorities to recreate the scene. Photographs are a permanent record of the terminal event and retain evidentiary value and authenticity. It is essential that the investigator obtain accurate photographs before releasing the scene.

2. Develop Descriptive Documentation of the Scene

Principle: Written documentation of the scene provides a permanent record that may be used to correlate with and enhance photographic documentation, refresh recollections and record observations.

Authorization: Medical Examiner/Coroner Official Office Policy Manual; State or Federal Statutory Authority.

Policy: Investigators shall provide written scene documentation.

Procedure: After photographic documentation of the scene and prior to removal of the body or other evidence, the investigator should:

A. Diagram/describe in writing items of evidence and their relationship to the body with necessary measurements.

B. Describe and document, with necessary measurements, blood and body fluid evidence, including volume, patterns, spatters and other characteristics.

C. Describe scene environments, including odors, lights, temperatures and other fragile evidence.

Note: If scene conditions have changed or evidence has been moved prior to written documentation, it should be noted in the report.

Summary: Written scene documentation is essential to correlate with photographic evidence and to re-create the scene for police, forensic(s), and judicial and civil agencies with a legitimate interest.

3. Establish Probable Location of Injury or Illness

Principle: The location where the decedent is found may not be the actual location where the injury/illness that contributed to the death occurred. It is imperative that the investigator attempt to determine the locations of any and all injury(ies)/illness(es) that may have contributed to the death. Physical evidence at any and all locations may be pertinent in establishing the cause, manner and circumstances of death.

Authorization: Medical Examiner/Coroner Official Office Policy Manual; State or Federal Statutory Authority.

Policy: The investigator shall obtain detailed information regarding any and all probable locations associated with the individual's death.

Procedure: The investigator should:

A. Document the location where death was confirmed.

B. Determine the location from which the decedent was transported and how the body was transported to the scene.

C. Identify and record discrepancies between the body and the scene (e.g., rigor mortis, livor mortis and body temperature).

D. Check the body, clothing and scene for consistency/inconsistency of trace evidence and indicate the location where artifacts are found.

E. Check for drag marks (on body and ground).

F. Establish post-injury activity.

G. Obtain dispatch (e.g., police, ambulance) record(s).

H. Interview family members and associates as needed.

Summary: Due to post-injury survival, advances in emergency medical services, multiple modes of transportation, the availability of specialized care, or criminal activity, a body may be moved from the actual location of illness/injury to a remote site. It is imperative that the investigator attempt to determine any and all locations where the decedent has previously been and the mode of transport from these sites.

4. Collect, Inventory and Safeguard Property and Evidence

Principle: The decedent's valuables/property must be safeguarded to ensure proper processing and eventual return to next of kin. Evidence on or near the body must be safeguarded to ensure its availability for further evaluation.

Authorization: Medical Examiner/Coroner Official Office Policy Manual; State or Federal Statutory Authority.

Policy: The investigator shall ensure that all property and evidence are collected, inventoried, safeguarded and released as required by law.

Procedure: After personal property and evidence have been identified at the scene, the investigator (with a witness) should:

A. Inventory, collect and safeguard illicit drugs and paraphernalia at the scene and office.

B. Inventory, collect and safeguard prescription medication at the scene and office.

C. Inventory, collect and safeguard over-the-counter medications at the scene and office.

D. Inventory, collect and safeguard money at the scene and office.

E. Inventory, collect, and safeguard personal valuables/property at the scene and office.

Summary: Personal property and evidence are important items at a death investigation. Evidence must be safeguarded to ensure its availability if needed for future evaluation and litigation.

Personal property must be safeguarded to ensure its eventual distribution to appropriate agencies or individuals and to reduce the likelihood that the investigator will be accused of stealing property.

5. Interview Witness(es) at the Scene

Principle: The documented comments of witnesses at the scene allow the investigator to obtain primary source data regarding discovery of the body, witness corroboration and terminal history. The documented interview provides essential information for the investigative process.

Authorization: Medical Examiner/Coroner Official Office Policy Manual; State or Federal Statutory Authority.

Policy: The investigator's report shall include the source of information, including specific statements and information provided by the witness.

Procedure: Upon arriving at the scene, the investigator should:

A. Collect all available identifying data on witness(es) (e.g., full name, address, date of birth, contact information).

B. Establish the witness's relationship/ association to the deceased.

C. Establish the basis of the witness's knowledge (how does the witness have knowledge of the death?).

D. Obtain information from each witness individually or as appropriate.

E. Note discrepancies from the scene briefing (challenge, explain, verify statements).

F. Record and retain statements as needed.

Summary: The investigator's final report must document the witness's identity and must include a summary of the witness's statements, corroboration with other witnesses and the circumstances of discovery of the death. This documentation must exist as a permanent record to establish a chain of events.

Section D:

Documenting and Evaluating the Body

1. Photograph the Body

Principle: The photographic documentation of the body at the scene creates a permanent record that preserves essential details of the body position, appearance, identity and final movements. Photographs allow sharing of information with other agencies investigating the death.

Authorization: Medical Examiner/Coroner Official Office Policy Manual; State or Federal Statutory Authority.

Policy: The investigator shall obtain detailed photographic documentation of the body that provides both instant and permanent high-quality images.

Procedure: Upon arrival at the scene, and prior to moving the body or evidence, the investigator should:

    A. Photograph the body and immediate scene (including the decedent as initially found).

    B. Photograph the decedent's face (never clean face, do not change condition).

    C. Take additional photographs after removal of objects/items that interfere with photographic documentation of the decedent (e.g., body removed from car).

    D. Photograph the decedent with and without measurements (as appropriate).

E. Photograph the surface beneath the body (after the body has been removed, as appropriate).

Note: Take multiple photographs if possible.

Summary: The photographic documentation of the body at the scene provides for documentation of the body position, identity and appearance. The details of the body at the scene provide investigators with pertinent information of the terminal events.

2. Conduct External Body Examination (Superficial)

Principle: Conducting the external body examination provides the investigator with objective data regarding the single most important piece of evidence at the scene, the body. This documentation provides detailed information regarding the decedent's physical attributes, his/her relationship to the scene, and possible cause, manner and circumstances of death.

Authorization: Medical Examiner/Coroner Official Office Policy Manual; State or Federal Statutory Authority.

Policy: The investigator shall obtain detailed photographs and written documentation of the decedent at the scene.

Procedure: After arrival at the scene and prior to moving the decedent, the investigator should, without removing the decedent's clothing:

A. Photograph the scene, including the decedent as initially found and the surface beneath the body after the body has been removed.

B. Photograph the decedent with and without measurements (as appropriate), including a photograph of the decedent's face.

C. Document the decedent's position with and without measurements (as appropriate).

D. Document the decedent's physical characteristics.

E. Document the presence, absence and condition of clothing and personal effects.

F. Document the presence or absence of any items/objects that may be relevant.

G. Document the presence or absence of marks, scars and tattoos.

H. Document the presence or absence of injury/trauma, petechiae, etc.

I. Document the presence of treatment or resuscitative efforts.

J. Based on the findings, determine the need for further evaluation/assistance of forensic specialists or technologies (e.g., pathologists, odontologists, alternate light sources).

Note: If necessary, take additional photographs after removal of objects/items that interfere with photographic documentation of the decedent.

Summary: Thorough evaluation and documentation (photographic and written) of the deceased at the scene are essential to determine the depth and direction the investigation will take.

3. Preserve Evidence (on Body)

Principle: The photographic and written documentation of evidence on the body allows the investigator to obtain a permanent historical record of that evidence. To maintain chain of custody, evidence must be documented, collected, preserved and transported properly. In addition to all of the physical evidence visible on the body, blood and other body fluids present must be photographed and documented prior to collection and transport. Fragile evidence (which can be easily contaminated, lost or altered) must also be collected and preserved to maintain chain of custody and to assist in determination of cause, manner and circumstances of death.

Authorization: Medical Examiner/Coroner Official Office Policy Manual; State or Federal Statutory Authority.

Policy: With photographic and written documentation, the investigator will provide a permanent record of evidence that is on the body.

Procedure: Once evidence on the body is recognized, the investigator should:

A. Photograph the evidence.

B. Document blood/body fluid on the body (e.g., froth/purge, substances from orifices), location and pattern before transporting.

C. Secure decedent's hands and feet in unused paper bags (as determined by the scene).

D. Identify and collect trace evidence before transporting the body (e.g., blood, hair, fibers).

E. Arrange for the collection and transport of evidence at the scene (when necessary).

F. Ensure the proper collection of blood and body fluids for subsequent analysis (if the body will be released from the scene to an outside agency without an autopsy).

Summary: It is essential that evidence be collected, preserved, transported and documented in an orderly and proper fashion to ensure the chain of custody and admissibility in a legal action. The preservation and documentation of the evidence on the body must be initiated by the investigator at the scene to prevent altera- tions or contamination. In some instances, identification of trace evidence may require al- ternative methods (e.g., alternate light source, presumptive testing).

4. Establish Decedent Identification

Principle: The establishment or confirmation of the decedent's identity is paramount to the death investigation. Proper identification allows no- tification of next of kin, settlement of estates, resolution of criminal and civil litigation, and the proper completion of the death certificate.

Authorization: Medical Examiner/Coroner Official Office Policy Manual; State or Federal Statutory Authority.

Policy: The investigator shall engage in a diligent effort to establish/confirm the decedent's identity.

Procedure: To establish identity, the investigator should document use of the following methods:

A. Direct visual or photographic identification of the decedent if visually recognizable (when authorized, a face may be cleaned to allow for identification after the initial photographic documentation is completed).

B. Scientific methods such as fingerprints and dental, radiographic and DNA comparisons.

C. Circumstantial methods such as (but not restricted to) personal effects, circumstances, physical characteristics, tattoos and anthropologic data.

Use available technologies to assist in decedent identification (e.g., www.namus.gov, National Crime Information Center).

Summary: There are several methods available that can be used to properly identify deceased persons. In some cases, the investigator should employ more than one method to confirm the identity of decedents. An autopsy along with authenticated in-dwelling medical devices may also be used to confirm identification. This is essential for investigative, judicial, family and vital records issues.

5. Document Post-Mortem Changes

Principle: The documenting of post-mortem changes to the body assists the investigator in explaining body appearance in the interval following death. Inconsistencies between post-mortem changes and body location may indicate movement of the body and validate or invalidate witness statements. In addition, post-mortem changes to the body, when correlated with circumstantial information, can assist the investigators in estimating the approximate time and location of death.

Authorization: Medical Examiner/Coroner Official Office Policy Manual; State or Federal Statutory Authority.

Policy: The investigator shall document all post-mortem changes relative to the decedent and the environment.

Procedure: Upon arrival at the scene and prior to moving the body, the investigator should note the presence of each of the following in his/her report:

    A. Livor (e.g., color, location, blanchability, Tardieu spots) consistent/inconsistent with position of the body.

    B. Rigor (e.g., stage/intensity, location on the body, broken, inconsistent with the scene).

    C. Degree of decomposition (e.g., putrefaction, adipocere, mummification, skeletonization, as appropriate).

    D. Insect and animal activity.

    E. Scene temperature (document method used and time estimated).

    F. Description of body temperature (e.g., warm, cold, frozen) or measurement of body temperature (document method used and time of measurement).

Summary: Documentation of post-mortem changes in every report is essential to determine an accurate cause and manner of death, provide information as to the time of death, corroborate witness statements, and indicate that the body may have been moved after death.

6. Participate in Scene Debriefing

Principle: The scene debriefing helps investigators from all participating agencies to establish post-scene responsibilities by sharing data regarding particular scene findings. The scene debriefing provides each agency the opportunity for input regarding special requests for assistance, additional information, special examinations, and other requests requiring interagency communication, cooperation and education.

Authorization: Medical Examiner/Coroner Official Office Policy Manual; State or Federal Statutory Authority.

Policy: The investigator shall participate in or initiate an interagency scene debriefing to verify specific post-scene responsibilities.

Procedure: When participating in scene debriefing, the investigator should:

A. Determine post-scene responsibilities (e.g., identification, notification, media relations and evidence transportation).

B. Determine/identify the need for a specialist (e.g., crime laboratory technicians, social services, entomologists, Occupational Safety and Health Administration).

C. Communicate with the pathologist about responding to the scene or to determine the autopsy schedule (as needed).

D. Share investigative data (as required in furtherance of the investigation), for example, to disclose the possible existence of communicable diseases.

E. Communicate special requests to appropriate agencies, being mindful of the necessity for confidentiality.

Summary: The scene debriefing is the best opportunity for investigative participants to communicate special requests and confirm all current and additional scene responsibilities. The debriefing allows participants the opportunity to establish clear lines of responsibility for a successful investigation. Complete processing of the scene may require an extended period of time beyond the initial scene investigation. This should be communicated between agencies beyond the initial scene, and investigators from different agencies need to stay in communication with each other throughout the entire time.

7. Determine Notification Procedures (Next of Kin or Interested and Authorized Individuals)

Principle: Every reasonable effort should be made to notify the next of kin or interested and authorized individuals as soon as possible. Notification of next of kin or interested and authorized individuals initiates the disposition of remains and facilitates the exchange of additional information relative to the case.

Authorization: Medical Examiner/Coroner Official Office Policy Manual; State or Federal Statutory Authority.

Policy: The investigator shall ensure that the next of kin or interested and authorized individuals are notified of the death and that all failed and successful attempts at notification are documented.

Procedure: When determining notification procedures, the investigator should:

A. Identify the next of kin or interested and authorized individuals (determine who will perform this task).

B. Locate the next of kin or interested and authorized individuals (determine who will perform this task).

C. Notify the next of kin or interested and authorized individuals (assign person(s) to perform this task) and record time of notification, or, if delegated to another agency, obtain and document confirmation when notification is made.

D. Notify interested and authorized agencies of status of the notification.

Summary: The investigator is responsible for ensuring that the next of kin or interested and authorized individuals are identified, located and notified in a timely manner. The time and method of notification should be documented. Failure to locate the next of kin or interested and authorized individuals and efforts to do so should be a matter of record. This ensures that every reasonable effort has been made to contact the family or interested and authorized individuals. When possible, notification should be performed in person.

8. Ensure Security of Remains

Principle: Ensuring security of the body requires the investigator to supervise the labeling, packaging and removal of the remains. An appropriate identification tag is placed on the body to preclude misidentification upon receipt at the examining agency. This function also includes safeguarding all potential physical evidence and property and clothing that remain on the body.

Authorization: Medical Examiner/Coroner Official Office Policy Manual; State or Federal Statutory Authority.

Policy: The investigator shall supervise and ensure the proper identification, inventory, and security of evidence/property and its packaging and removal from the scene.

Procedure: Prior to leaving the scene, the investigator should:

A. Ensure that the body is protected from further trauma or contamination (if not, document) and unauthorized removal of therapeutic and resuscitative equipment.

B. Inventory and secure property, clothing and personal effects that are on the body (remove in a controlled environment with a witness present).

C. Identify property and clothing to be retained as evidence (in a controlled environment).

D. Recover biological samples before releasing the remains.

E. Place identification on the body and body bag.

F. Ensure/supervise the placement of the body into the bag and secure it.

G. Ensure/supervise the removal of the body from the scene.

H. Secure transportation.

Summary: Ensuring the security of the remains facilitates proper identification of the remains, maintains a proper chain of custody, and safeguards property and evidence.

Establishing and Recording Decedent Profile Information

1. Document the Discovery History

Principle: Establishing a decedent profile includes documenting a discovery history and circumstances surrounding the discovery. The basic profile will dictate subsequent levels of investigation, jurisdiction and authority. The focus (breadth/depth) of further investigation is dependent on this information.

Authorization: Medical Examiner/Coroner Official Office Policy Manual; State or Federal Statutory Authority.

Policy: The investigator shall document the discovery history, available witnesses and apparent circumstances leading to death.

Procedure: For an investigator to correctly document the discovery history, he/she should:

A. Establish and record person(s) who discovered the body and when.

B. Document the circumstances surrounding the discovery (who, what, where, when, how).

Summary: The investigator must produce clear, concise, documented information concerning who discovered the body, what the circumstances of discovery were, where the discovery occurred, when the discovery was made and how the discovery was made.

2. Determine Terminal Episode History

Principle: Preterminal circumstances play a significant role in determining cause and manner of death. Documentation of medical intervention and procurement of antemortem specimens help to establish the decedent's condition prior to death.

Authorization: Medical Examiner/Coroner Official Office Policy Manual; State or Federal Statutory Authority.

Policy: The investigator shall document known circumstances and medical intervention preceding death.

Procedure: In order for the investigator to determine terminal episode history, he/she should:

    A. Document when, where, how and by whom the decedent was last known to be alive.

    B. Document the incidents prior to the death.

    C. Document complaints/symptoms prior to the death.

    D. Document and review complete EMS records.

    E. Obtain relevant medical and pharmacy records.

    F. Obtain relevant antemortem specimens.

Summary: Obtaining records of preterminal circumstances and medical history distinguishes medical treatment from trauma. The history, relevant antemortem specimens, and electronic data collected and/or transmitted may assist the medical examiner/coroner in determining cause and manner of death.

3. Document Decedent Medical History

Principle: The majority of deaths referred to the medical examiner/coroner are natural deaths. Establishing the decedent's medical history helps to focus the investigation. Documenting the decedent's medical signs or symptoms prior to death determines the need for subsequent examinations. The relationship between disease and injury may play a role in the cause, manner and circumstances of death.

Authorization: Medical Examiner/Coroner Official Office Policy Manual; State or Federal Statutory Authority.

Policy: The investigator shall obtain the decedent's past medical history.

Procedure: Through interviews and review of the written records, the investigator should:

    A. Document medical history, including medications obtained and taken, alcohol and drug use, and family medical history, including alternative practices.

    B. Document information from treating physicians and/or hospitals to confirm history and treatment.

    C. Document physical characteristics and traits (e.g., left-/right-handedness, missing appendages, tattoos, implanted/indwelling devices, etc.).

Summary: Obtaining a thorough medical history focuses the investigation, aids in disposition of the case, and helps determine the need for a post-mortem examination or other laboratory tests or studies. Potential sources of medical information should include but are not limited to nursing homes, hospice agencies, intermediate care, and assisted living facilities.

Electronic media can be a valuable source of information for obtaining a decedent's medical history.

4. Document Decedent Mental Health History

Principle: The decedent's mental health history can provide insight into the behavior/state of mind of the individual. That insight may produce clues that will aid in establishing the cause, manner and circumstances of the death.

Authorization: Medical Examiner/Coroner Official Office Policy Manual; State or Federal Statutory Authority.

Policy: The investigator shall obtain information from sources familiar with the decedent pertaining to the decedent's mental health history.

Procedure: The investigator should attempt to:

A. Document the decedent's mental health history, including behavioral issues, hospitalizations and medications.

B. Document the history of suicidal ideations, gestures and/or attempts.

C. Document mental health professionals (e.g., psychiatrists, psychologists, counselors) who treated the decedent.

D. Document family mental health history.

E. Obtain relevant records.

Summary: Knowledge of the mental health history allows the investigator to properly evaluate the decedent's state of mind and contributes to the determination of cause, manner and circumstances of death.

5. Document Social History

Principle: Social history includes marital, family, sexual, educational, employment and financial information. Daily routines, habits and activities, and friends and associates of the decedent help in developing the decedent's profile. This information will aid in establishing the cause, manner and circumstances of death.

Authorization: Medical Examiner/Coroner Official Office Policy Manual; State or Federal Statutory Authority.

Policy: The investigator shall obtain social history information from sources familiar with the decedent.

Procedure: When collecting relevant social history information, the investigator should:

A. Document marital/domestic history.

B. Document family history (similar deaths, significant dates).

C. Document sexual history.

D. Document employment history.

E. Document financial history.

F. Document daily routines, habits, activities, hobbies and unusual behavioral patterns.

G. Document Internet activity (e.g., social media sites).

H. Document relationships, friends, caregivers and associates.

I. Document religious, ethnic or other pertinent information (e.g., religious objection to autopsy).

J. Document educational background.

K. Document criminal history and obtain relevant records.

Summary: Information from sources familiar with the decedent pertaining to the decedent's social history assists in the determination of cause, manner and circumstances of death. Special attention may be required in dependent populations (e.g., infants, special needs and the elderly).

Completing the Scene Investigation

1. Maintain Jurisdiction Over the Body

Principle: Maintaining jurisdiction over the body allows the investigator to protect the chain of custody as the body is transported from the scene for autopsy, specimen collection or storage.

Authorization: Medical Examiner/Coroner Official Office Policy Manual; State or Federal Statutory Authority.

Policy: The investigator shall maintain jurisdiction of the body by arranging for the body to be transported for autopsy, specimen collection or storage by secure conveyance.

Procedure: When maintaining jurisdiction over the body, the investigator should:

A. Arrange for, and document, secure transportation of the body to a medical or autopsy facility for further examination or storage.

B. Coordinate and document procedures to be performed when the body is received at the facility.

Summary: By providing documented secure transportation of the body from the scene to an authorized receiving facility, the investigator maintains jurisdiction and protects chain of custody of the body.

2. Release Jurisdiction of the Body

Principle: Prior to releasing jurisdiction of the body to an authorized receiving agent or funeral director, it is necessary to determine the person responsible for certification of the death. Information to complete the death certificate includes demographic information and the date, time and location of death.

Authorization: Medical Examiner/Coroner Official Office Policy Manual; State or Federal Statutory Authority.

Policy: The investigator shall obtain sufficient data to enable completion of the death certificate and release of jurisdiction over the body.

Procedure: When releasing jurisdiction over the body, the investigator should:

A. Determine who will sign the death certificate (name, agency, etc.).

B. Confirm the date, time and location of death.

C. Collect, when appropriate, biological samples and other evidence prior to release of the body (indwelling or implanted devices).

D. Document and arrange with the authorized receiving agent to reconcile all death certificate information.

E. Release the body to an authorized funeral director, medical examiner/coroner or other authorized receiving agent.

Summary: The investigator releases jurisdiction only after determining who will sign the death certificate; documenting the date, time and location of death; collecting appropriate specimens;

and releasing the body to the authorized funeral director or other authorized receiving agent.

3. Perform Exit Procedures

Principle: Completion of the scene investigation ensures that important evidence has been collected and the scene has been processed. In addition, a systematic review of the scene ensures that artifacts or equipment are not inadvertently left behind and any dangerous materials or conditions have been reported and documented.

Authorization: Medical Examiner/Coroner Official Office Policy Manual; State or Federal Statutory Authority.

Policy: At the conclusion of the scene investigation, the investigator shall conduct a post-investigative "walk through" and ensure the scene investigation is complete.

Procedure: When performing exit procedures, the investigator should:

A. Identify, inventory and remove all evidence collected at the scene.

B. Remove all personal equipment and materials from the scene.

C. Report and document any dangerous materials or conditions.

D. Alert family or interested and authorized individuals to potential unsafe scene conditions.

Summary: Conducting a scene "walk through" upon exit ensures that all evidence has been collected,

that materials are not inadvertently left behind, and that any dangerous materials or
conditions have been documented and
reported to the proper entities.

4. Assist the Family or Authorized Individual(s)

Principle: The investigator provides the family or authorized individual(s) with a timetable so they can
arrange for final disposition and provides information on available community and professional resources that may assist the family.

Authorization: Medical Examiner/Coroner Official Office
Policy Manual; State or Federal Statutory
Authority.

Policy: The investigator shall offer the decedent's
family or authorized individual(s) information
regarding available community and professional resources.

Procedure: When the investigator is assisting the family
or authorized individual(s), it is important to:

A. Inform them if an autopsy is required.

B. Inform them of available support services
(e.g., victim assistance, police, social services, death scene cleanup).

C. Inform them of appropriate agencies to
contact with questions (e.g., medical
examiner/coroner offices, law enforcement, SIDS support group, etc.).

D. Ensure that the family or authorized
individual(s) is not left alone with the
body (if circumstances warrant).

E. Inform them of the approximate body
release timetable.

F. Inform them of the information release timetable (e.g., toxicology, autopsy results, as required).

G. Inform them of available reports, including cost, if any.

H. Inform them that they might be contacted regarding organ and tissue donation.

I. Inform them that they may receive inquiries from the media (this will be case dependent).

Summary: Interaction with the family or authorized individual(s) allows the investigator to assist and direct them to appropriate resources. It is essential that families or authorized individual(s) be given a timetable of events so that they can make necessary arrangements. In addition, the investigator needs to communicate what information will be available and an approximate timeline for its release.

About the National Institute of Justice

The National Institute of Justice — the research, development and evaluation agency of the Department of Justice — is dedicated to improving our knowledge and understanding of crime and justice issues through science. NIJ provides objective and independent knowledge and tools to reduce crime and promote justice, particularly at the state and local levels.

NIJ's pursuit of this mission is guided by the following principles:

- Research can make a difference in individual lives, in the safety of communities and in creating a more effective and fair justice system.

- Government-funded research must adhere to processes of fair and open competition guided by rigorous peer review.

- NIJ's research agenda must respond to the real world needs of victims, communities and criminal justice professionals.

- NIJ must encourage and support innovative and rigorous research methods that can provide answers to basic research questions as well as practical, applied solutions to crime.

- Partnerships with other agencies and organizations, public and private, are essential to NIJ's success.

Our principal authorities are derived from:

- The Omnibus Crime Control and Safe Streets Act of 1968, amended (see 42 USC §§ 3721-3723)

- Title II of the Homeland Security Act of 2002

- Justice For All Act, 2004

To find out more about the National Institute of Justice, please visit:

www.nij.gov

or contact:

National Criminal Justice References Service
P.O. Box 6000
Rockville, MD 20849-6000
800-851-3420
www.ncjrs.gov

The National Institute of Justice is a component of the Office of Justice Programs, which also includes the Bureau of Assistance; the Bureau of Justice Statistics; the Community Capacity Development Office; the Office for Victims of Crime; the Office of Juvenile Justice and Delinquency Prevention; and the Office of Sex Offender Sentencing, Monitoring, Apprehending, Registering, and Tracking (SMART).

www.ingramcontent.com/pod-product-compliance
Lightning Source LLC
Chambersburg PA
CBHW070615290526
45790CB00002B/924